It's Easy to Lose Your Breath

It's Easy to Lose Your Breath

poems

Kevin A. Risner

Chicago | Los Angeles

It's Easy to Lose Your Breath

Copyright © 2026 by Kevin A. Risner

All rights reserved.

Published in the United States by Match Factory Editions, 2026

ISBN 978-1-966253-22-8 (hardcover)
ISBN 978-1-966253-23-5 (paperback)
ISBN 978-1-966253-21-1 (ebook)

Library of Congress Control Number: 2026938581

matchfactoryeditions.com

Book layout by RD Morgan

Cover art and design by Gretchen Hasse

Colophon design by Randy Cochran

TABLE OF CONTENTS

I.

We Never Thought It Would Ever Happen

What If I Told You Lemon Trees Once Existed?

A sixth extinction has come at the end
of the 21st century, has passed.
Brains float on top of soup ready for us
to skim. The headlines, all over the place,
make proclamation that winter solstice is gone,
won't come back. Bright yellow discs appear,
bobbing on the surface of every single glass
as the sun peeks out and the tart lies of summer
never leave. Even on Friday the 13th. Somehow luckier
now with each new virus wedged into the world,
leaving ghost towns in their wake. Alive or asleep,
it doesn't matter how we go about this next phase
of existence. Morning calls, and I find a tuxedo,
put on sunglasses to face this godforsaken world.
I'll take the nearest bike and crash into the swimming pool
and wait for the next eclipse to finish us off.

Bloodbuzz

You know, there's no space
left for me on this planet.

I'm sitting cross-legged
for the zillionth time.

In my scotch-clogged brain
I can zipper my lips,

foist the ear trumpet
against the wall to enjoy the symphony.

Patience, locust. It'll all even out
after the bombs have dropped.

It's no earthquake.
It's no picnic.

Here we have the same bastards
we've voted in again

who will fan the flames
as I fan my face in blistering July.

The next month always comes so fast.

A Golden Retriever Chases Me During My Five-Mile
Run

time keeps me in a bending pose
I wait for it to go away

it finds me by the medium
and I run until I can't go any farther

who knew that if I stopped running
the thing chasing me could stop too

the fear dissolving
the instant I stopped and took a breath

Lungs

when I learn of stories about some of my relatives
from a time that involved clawing their way
through the coal mines of Pennsylvania
I hold my breath to feel the shrinking of my airways

my brain flickers back to grade school
I'd been asked to run the 400 without training
and I tried to sprint and something happened
the inability to bring what I needed into me

the way to survive is involuntary
like the shaking away of the fallen snow
from hats and tree limbs and other
unexpected surfaces too numerous to count

abridged versions of novels were OK back then
but I want the entire thing
ready for me to dive into to forget about
my breathing for a while

how can one be dispirited when looking
at an octopus in the water, curious for a whole minute
I'd been watering my shoes for 40 minutes
without noticing I've produced the next flood

During the First Year of the Pandemic, a Frog Snuck
into the House

Our only visitor for months and months and months. We transported it
to a cool, shaded location in our backyard, and it didn't take long for it to
bound away and disappear. We never could tell whether the croaking we
heard after dark was partly our guest. It lulled us to sleep – like a talisman
in the havoc of that year. As I think about our frog visitor today, I still
don't know how it got in. But we never really know when something
sneaks inside. And the surprise when we find it might just be what we
need.

A Blue Jay Flies into the Window

I see my reflection where I never expected it. One of my good friends brings scotch to celebrate our birthdays. We pull our masks down only for sips as we sit in beach chairs beneath the magnolia past blossom – the one high point before everything falls apart at the end of the month. From the bedroom, I hear the thud. As if someone was angry and had thrown something at our home. There's a splotch on the window. I run into the backyard, and I see cerulean motionless on the stones. If I give it a nudge, it'll move. It has to. Beneath one of the maple trees, I open up the earth to put the bird inside. When done, I nudge the jay onto the spade of the shovel. No reaction but gravity. I'm the only human who weeps for this lone songbird. Dirt over the grave. Quickly. It stays where it is. I stay where I am. I take a long breath. Let the shovel fall. Look up at an endlessly blue sky.

We're Humming Al Green Songs as We Get Ready for
Bed

During one opening note,
we sigh and exhale.
After our first dance

back in 2015,
"Let's Stay Together"
invited others

to join us on the wood-paneled floor.
Swerve, lean, circle around, croon.
Now, you peer at me through the mirror

as you brush your teeth.
I lie in bed playing at reading,
a casual reflection on middle-age habits

in the time of Covid.
We never thought it would ever happen:
there would be a smudge of red skies,

wind, asphalt summers, plum
trees dropping fruit throughout
my grandmother's backyard.

You know, as a kid, I mowed around
those plums every week, ate Whopper Juniors
with her when I was finished.

That 1998 heat was so oppressive,
like books stacked on top of one another.
Mary, as soon as you can,

let's melt this summer
form into something magnetic and bright –
you'll always be my greatest dream.

Another Visitor

On the lowest step on the way to the basement, a spider has spun its story for months until it has to move to a spot beside the house, the ferns curling up like wildfire, a central opening for a new web. I place it there and let it be. Five hours later, there's a scuttle in the underbrush, home not yet built. But it always takes a while to settle in. The next day, thunder cracks and rains over an inch pummel asphalt and trees and wires, and we never see it again. But there are no floods or standing water anywhere in that part of the yard. So I'm hoping for the best.

Zoom Cards Against Humanity

A group of us sit around, but the table isn't circular.
We have options like usual, and we choose the funniest ones,
the dirtiest, the most accurate fill-in-the-blanks

to this ridiculous situation we find ourselves in.
When I speak, my whole self is highlighted.
Everyone sees a large enhancement of me:

unkempt, insular, interior. I pop up for a few seconds.
This situation has left me eating rice and beans. Perhaps
a new curry with seventy photos on the webpage:

a novella and the tiniest square of directions at the end.
If I'm feeling nostalgic, I'll learn beer bread.
We also eat spaghetti squash during one of the game nights,

and everyone thought it was pasta. That's all
we're eating during quarantine. Don a bib, wait
for more. A slug of arak and some Oreos we nabbed

from a store we won't name because we don't want to
let the truth out. It seems almost everyone is Zooming
for everything now. For work, for meetups with friends,

for family check-ins. Any program similar to Zoom.
To see faces — familiar, kind faces at the present — sates us
for a short while. A satisfying escape from bitter reality.

Everything in Its Right Place

Parasite is my last movie
in the theater before the coronavirus
shuts them down. I lose my job
a few months after that.

                        We're still
locked down and wondering how
people could open their mouths
with all this anxiety falling like rain,
flooding in the knowledge
I know nothing but fear.

Everything in its right place,
I say as I sweep the windows
away.

        The ants always return,
and I'm always the one
who sees them first.

House Finches

Working from home brought me a closeup view of house finches making a nest on the deck between the sconce and the brick wall of our house. From April to Memorial Day we were not allowed to hang out as their fledglings appeared. In the midst of the pandemic, watching them was an obsession, and I prayed no blue jay would disrupt the nest as the parents foraged, a lookout always on our market umbrella. Eventually, it was time for the brood to spread their wings, flutter madly to get the right propulsion, make it to the deck railings before ungracefully flying away. That next winter, I learned from our neighbors that a hawk had slammed a small songbird against the window overlooking their backyard. And my prayer is that it had not been one of those finches, unsuspecting, at the feeder. How exposed they were that year, had we been that year, as we tried to surface from an Omicron wave. We wanted everything to get back to normal, the next obsession, when we still felt very much like sitting ducks.

Sisyphus

torture is

        shoveling
snow an hour into the squall

the scraping over concrete mirrors a whittler
carving away decibels

                I begin to clear a way
out of the house
an hour before dawn

        and secret worlds pop up while coffee
wings throughout the crisp air

turns into fingers, taps my shoulder
to come back inside

the trickle from the pot like earache medicine

the first evening of winter is a free taste
of the afterlife
        I stick my toes in

scalding water, a test to see whether
I'll shout and hit the ceiling

I recline and remain immobile for 40 minutes
healing sinks into each muscle as I levitate

at the surface of teakettle water
   read *The Plague* with a highball glass of
     something on the ledge

the heat slowly ebbs until the one second
that leaves me
frozen because there's a draft from
        somewhere

I forget what season it is

the fog has returned
the howls, louder
a fresh coating
     stretches over everything
    right as I finish the backbreaking chore

gloves, boots, scarf, hat
all stretched out
resting by the heat vent
like a cat

they all wait for me to
go out and do it again

Ground

The ground is ice, hewn from glacier.
November mornings are a frozen fog.
Third-grade afternoons disappeared after the flurries started
falling. Everyone would shout exaltations to God.
We knew, but we heard and embraced the truth.
The early afternoon light was tempered
from some tinted corner. You know, I felt raw
when the worst of winter inched above the earth, fossilizing
the enormity of four frigid months to come.
It felt like a vast collection of sagas unread, untold,
not yet rolled out for the public to know, and soon to ingrain
in their subconscious. I held a fraction of the time I had
and what I yearned for was not enough to dredge the full
length of a year, thrummed into nothing, brined
like last year's turkey not yet defrosted but soon.
Once this machine has thawed from the initial freeze,
I wouldn't have felt it were possible if I didn't know
houses could bang because of 20-degree drops in temperature.
In January, all of the world stops moving
and I wish we knew the formula to get ourselves back.
Forgiving oneself is a labor of Hercules,
bringing what's left of a world that's been shuttered.

An Icy Triptych

Back when

The world fell

And I knew

Everything was lost

I kept swimming

In the lake

Until the ice formed

The sky grew dark

Into a roaring fire

It was the final day

In middle-of-spring fog

Even when I couldn't see

Breezes licking my ears

One last time

I loved it when I found out

Each paper-thin night

Before the past told me

Always pressed tightly

The lighthouse, on and alert

Exposed to the chills of all life

Before it stopped

April Tanka

whenever you go
bursting into bloom in spring
never forget me
sitting listless, with branches
bare and waiting to open

Hope

a red oak sapling
now in a watering can
soon in our front yard

We've Somehow Figured Out True Bliss

We've somehow figured out true bliss
on opposite ends of the couch
feet touching
reading lines out loud
to one another
any novel that's our favorite

Breadcrumbs

To follow a trail for what feels like miles,
the reward is in the journey but also what's found,

the breadcrumbs fresher than an eight a.m. bakery,
so whoever was here was here only minutes before.

Find them. Just another curve,
just another bend. Deeper into the forest,

and the hidden nook will swell like rosebushes in summer.
Cast a net for the first swarm. Anyone can catch them,

find whoever rained manna from a basket.
Might have to crawl along, smudge knees,

collect earth in clumps like a geologist.
The early evening gloom has a sentience.

A breath here, a breath there, but none from oneself.
Hold it longer than a parental hand.

It's only the wind, even when the leaves are still
as death. Find the one who lures people in here

to wherever the pathway ends. This is a narrative
told daily, in one's head. No one else ahead,

no person with a basket to drop what one needs
to survive. Nothing else but a hoot, a hint, an inkling

that there's something else in the leaves ready to appear.
With one more step, with one more breath, with one more –

II.

The Pandemic Diaries

My dreams involve walking through doors and into buildings, suffocating. The air slinks upward. I can't go there. All I can do is look up to see the vaulted ceiling peppered with orbs that hum orange and yellow, as if I've released all the tapioca spheres from boba tea and left them to levitate for eternity. My mind is a blur as the oxygen gets depleted, as if I truly did get sick and the most recent actions I've taken are now lost in a giant warehouse with numberless aisles. Each turn down the next one sets off alarms that release rebar from supports. It's impossible to avoid them as I go from aisle to aisle. I'm lost. I can't balance myself with all of these obstacles. I'm gasping for air, trying to surface. And I don't have the inhaler I'd relied on so heavily in high school.

*

A former student of mine informed me during the previous Lunar New Year celebration that I'd need to brace myself for my year – The Year of the Rat – for major life changes might occur: marriage, a new child, death, something else just as potent. She did not say exactly what I must do to prepare, simply that I'd have to be ready for whatever would be on the horizon.

*.

In late January, a few students disappear for a week, some for two weeks or more. They meekly return, a few with deep chest coughs. One of them tells me he was the sickest he'd ever been in his life. He felt like he was dying, thought he was actually going to die. A colleague reaches out on Facebook some time in early February, asking whether anyone else has noticed a greater number of sick students this semester. Many people chime in with yeses. My wife encounters some of her students from China coming to class in masks. It had been a normal occurrence for years, so it often wouldn't cause us to blink twice. This time, we know it's different.

*

I tell everyone in my classes at the start of March, "see you after Spring Break!" At one of the schools where I adjunct, some students were studying abroad in Italy, and they returned sooner than anticipated. In hindsight, I wonder if I should have said that cheery phrase to my classes before the week we'd be away. The following Tuesday, our state shuts down because Covid has officially made it into Ohio. Even though it had been here. All schools go completely virtual. And I never see these students in person ever again.

*

I'm building an entire Earth in my head, and it's just like this Earth. But not really. I mean, there's a lot of sky. A blistering sun, roaring waves, swirling hurricanes in the distance (but never landfalling). There's a range of unrelenting mountains, blue spruces covering the lower sections. There are chocolate Labrador retrievers bounding across sand, waves collapsing onto the shore but then returning to the ocean. Total solar eclipses pop up every other week. Everything is perfect.

*

My wife gives me a recipe for beer bread. She reminds me that it's easily accessible through email should I forget the necessary ingredients. I indulge in mornings full of carbs, coffee, scrolling newsfeeds, reading articles by Ed Yong about the pandemic.

*

Everyone wants to bake bread; everyone wants to make hummus; everyone wants to stockpile on toilet paper. I tell myself, if we fall into a world of even worse chaos some time in the near future, if we do indeed find ourselves on the other side of this coronavirus, there will be no space left for hope. Our collective empathy, already microscopic, will be impossible to find on any map. If we plunge into future wars, if there grows any sort of unrest, the only way out of it is a high vertical climb, the walls coated in oil, the floor lined with spikes.

*

I get a call from HR at the end of June. Starting the first of July, I have no full-time job. The call takes less than five minutes. I gather all of the names I can, try to save messages; I reach out to a few people, staff and faculty, old students. I tell them I'm not coming back in the fall. I don't go into detail.

*

But maybe I'll see you around?

*

More dreams of me indoors. I'm always indoors. I'm always wondering why I'm indoors. Why I'm so close to everyone. Why I'm not taking the necessary precautions. Why I've completely thrown everything against the wall. Why I'm just watching all of what I've thrown at the wall drip down, down, down – a masochistic form of doom-scrolling.

*

If I thought we'd be better after the first year, I was mistaken. If I thought
the air would get less murky the further along in life I'd go, I didn't bank
on another round of exhaust. The walls continue to rise, the sky continues
to thicken, and the dreams return. They bleed into morning. They're here
for me as I slink back into the unknown.

*

And so I return to that Earth I'd formed my head. I eradicate everything. The countries have borders, and I get mad. Why the hell did you outline them with borders, Kevin? Well, as a child, that's all I knew. That's what I did in sixth grade, too. I created a continent on wide-ruled notebook paper when I should have been doing classwork. I was a savvy makeshift cartographer. Each of my classmates' names were the countries' names. And then invasions happened. And the kids bordering me in class were intrigued. They wanted me to create a five-years-later map. Which countries would be gone, which ones would still exist? Which ones would grow into empires? And then, when would those empires inevitably collapse?

***

III.

Each Month Holds an Incredible Monster

When do you believe
the earth will be so heavy
it will sink every landmass into
ocean?
      Should the giant waves be seen
as a gift when they reach our doors?
I love the rhythmic roar in New Jersey
but not when it's ready to swallow
cars whole.
      Seriously, who gets to
tell us when it's the perfect time to clean
our plates, scrape every last morsel
into the depths of the sun?

A New Year Grows Its First Set of Teeth

We're back, another humble January, another horrible January, another glaring placemat full of shoes. I haven't bought anything new recently. I haven't lost anything new recently. So I breathe. There was a time I woke up before 6 a.m. I was teaching schoolchildren on the other side of the world, received poverty wage along with unemployment. Who knew my late 30s would be full of résumé-building and endless mugs of coffee? "We regret to inform you" – the famous first/last words. To regret. In the infinitive sense. Infinite, maybe. The number of AI teeth on that laughing human is uncountable. Indulge in sentience. Give it back. We didn't make food for the ball dropping. It's just us and no one else. Not even Janus. We walked on the towpath. One of these days was nothing like past Januarys. I realize I'm grinding molars, every single breathing second.

Alchemy

bodies turn into candles every winter / light the wick / right when light ever so slightly peeks out of uniform gray / a constant for the past month / dawn arrives with an alarm / teeth rattling before all creatures outside amble out of lairs / before fresh truths are revealed / run into the backyard / plaster minerals over every scrap of skin / a buffer against every insect / every creature one has yet to encounter / each month holds an incredible monster / and everything about the stark world drips like standing up after an hour-long bath / lava falling everywhere / on the table / the floor / through racks of wood / a caulking of sinew fat smoke / what is left of sound is food for the birds / the sky flicks into a new frame / the snow dons its final coat / one arm first / then the other / soon it will ready to leave / and then there will be nothing but nothing

It's Calm Tonight

The world has other ideas – whenever it gets the chance,
it paints the forest with lava. The path after it thickens,
it's the easiest, breath visible on Sunday morning winter hike –
and we know what's ahead but perhaps there are places
still too hot to touch. Poke around and see what's safe
and what's still molten, encapsulation of the present day,
ancient past, dystopia inching even closer.
And maybe a resurrection growing ever nearer.
The fog claims there's nothing more to see.

Post-Dusk

The two of us trudge down a path through the woods, the trees full and unbelievable. The sunset calls before we notice the dampening of the skies. Our legs kick at a fast-walk pace, even when the roots and undergrowth warn us: we shouldn't be walking fast. Minute after minute, the aura deepens, darkens. And we cling to one another as the trees grow taller, and we wonder what's hidden behind them. Which door do we choose? I wish there'd be a special threshold, a lane with nothing inside. Just the same pathway. We'd get to the car, and we'd go away. Hours earlier in the brash sun, we'd be transfixed, our hearts swelling. There'd be nothing, no glances behind, no views of the past, no wondering *what if we get stuck here before total darkness arrives?*

There's Always a Warm Spell in February

it's crept further north each year
and it's for longer each time
one of these days I'm going to get my lounge chair
get one of those trifold mirror reflectors and daub zinc
on my nose and beneath my eyes like a baseball player

just to prove a point

that I often look like a fool
like when I meandered around crowded spaces
in a mask and I pretended to cough as a tic
because maybe people wouldn't judge me as much
if they thought I was protecting them
from some vicious disease you know
since the ground hadn't frozen over yet
and all those viruses were flying around unfettered
unwilling to give it a rest already

After the Start of Summer

The lake blooms a bright green more vivid than geckos.
When these blooms enter the household, it's only natural
to collect them, place them in a glass vase, burn eyes
with pollen. Pink and orange petals flutter onto the table.

They say that algae blooms mean an overabundance
of phosphorus. It's toxic.

We drink up facts, reap the consequences, even when
it's not our fault. I am a wooden raft headed down
the river after a heavy rain. The water's thick there.

I hope to make my way out of this sand trap
through storm into sunlight, no longer
hidden by mattress-stuffing clouds in
the endless overcast that is November.

Jersey Shore Wildlife

I've spent most of my last few vacations
staring at sandpipers as they navigate the sand
right along the shoreline
the waves eating at their space
yet they continue pattering toward the tide line
and then run fast as hell in the other direction
as the next frothy stream comes along.

I buoy myself on a lounge chair
waiting for the crabs to rise up
poke around to make sure there's no one around
to halt their slow trudge back to the ocean
the pull of the tide not enough
to carry them out to sea
peeking out and realizing it's a mistake.

I pull out a magazine
and my pleasure reading winds up being
a long-form piece about wildfires out west
and the pine forests of Oregon and Washington
continually becoming smaller and smaller
because new growth can't grow that fast
and controlled burns are outstripped by other ones.

My new leisure activity is noticing ladybugs
rise up beneath the wet sand as if transported
from some barrier island, reappearing each day
I return to that stretch of Sea Isle City shore
while the previous year we made it to the cape

right as dragonflies blew by on their migration south
a constant zipping swarm unimpeded by anything.

The days are too few and the asphalt bakes
and I've grown to see earth as a magnet
drawing in tides and a sea level that's constantly clawing
away at the sand and the rocky soil and the tufts
of grass so unbearably green on the dune ridges
and I glance at a forecast graphic months later to see
this peninsula will be underwater in a few decades.

The Conch Republic

Members of this group
of snowbirds in Key West
burn a hurricane warning flag
at the end of the season
both a symbolic sigh of relief
and in memory of the lost
of the damage this year wrought.

If I make another map,
what would be included?
I draw another landform. Another island
in the shape of a seashell.
Press my ear against the paper
to hear the swirl of the ocean
to catch next year's forecast.

I may have bit off
more than I can chew.
Here we thought the 1990s was a time
of completely indisputable innocence.
A month after we left Florida
Hurricane Andrew ate away
the lower half of the state.

I've taken a deep breath in December
and have contracted an unknown virus.
Now, celebration is a morning that doesn't involve
phlegm or chest coughs or lozenges.
I've kept everyone safe. Now what?

The knowledge that I can try my best
and I might still fail.

It's Easy to Lose Your Breath

after The National

It's easy to mishear.
How often it's happened
as blue light echoes solitude at 2 a.m.

Ants crawl all over me
left over from the last time
an apocalypse ate cities
bone clean.

I've deftly avoided the world
for years now
and now I'm ready to fling everything
against the wall.

Each time I walk into a crowded place
the warring slide projectors hum and

it's 1997 again.

Jump through Time like a makeshift Dr. Who
like I've borrowed a DeLorean
for the evening.

I'm leaping through hoops, headed back,
I'll be surrounded by the sea
where it should never be.

I shouldn't be here.

I'll hold my breath and save it
for when I'm snorkeling through the corals
before they bleach
before the rainbow fish dart all around me
set off and never come back.

Ancient Burial Ground

They nailed a spike into the earth
to mark the ancient burial ground.

A sign reminds us to respect the dead,
not to step in certain spots.

We only seem to revere them all
once they're dead

gone from every facet of our lives
except for city and street names and sports teams

but their spirits frighten
even more than bodies would.

What will they do when they see
we resemble their killers?

So many people forget these places
and now spikes are pipes

that will run through the earth
stab the heart that sutures every soul together.

The First Apartment I Rented

Looking skyward was inevitable. Back then,
the blocks of apartments rolled with the terrain.
Concrete and stone covered every inch of earth.

My fear was wondering what might happen
to this complex if the future Great Istanbul Earthquake
struck sometime in the next month.

Pancaked ground floors commonplace
and, living on the story above, I blessed the armoire
in my cubbyhole of a bedroom.

The wardrobe would likely tilt over but not fully.
I praised how thin the room's layout was —
but would the above stories succumb to gravity,

crush me anyway if the Richter leapt over eight?
The next thought: Find out the building codes.
Does Bülent have them?

The only way to stay safe would be to lounge
on a retrofitted balcony lined with fake grass
high enough from Sea of Marmara tsunami,

an endless surge pushing ashore,
engulfing the rock walls and walkways
submerged at ten feet, at the very least.

What's tomorrow morning's devastation?
The transport to memory, the bitter patterns on the inner
edge of a coffee mug, lost granules of two decades ago

bringing foreseen waves, unbelievable destruction.
I now sit in a house thousands of miles away
and think about the next tornado outbreak here.

Summertime Sestina

I've heard enough shouts today
to last me all of July 4th week.
What's left to believe when everyone sits,
waits for each broken record to mend
tomorrow. I've scheduled ten minutes to sleep
in the afternoon, but not before five.

How many more years until we shrug off 9 to 5,
a crescent seat that's never seen the light of day?
Maybe there's nothing left to do but sleep
through the newsfeed, through the pain this week
but without having the ability to mend
whatever's left, the ulcer ripping, never sitting

still. Keep me hidden, so I'm not asked to babysit
the birds. The raucous starlings in multiples of five.
Sublimate the final note before we begin to mend
the couch's broken cushion, patch each yesterday
until nothing's left, only an eternally bewildering week
caught in a reckoning, an apocalypse asleep.

I've heard it's sometimes easy to sleep
in Michigan. You only hear the crickets as August sits
and waits for the newest voice, sounding weak,
sounding understanding. Who's left to claw at five a.m.
existentialism? God forbid we whittle away today.
It's not only me who's needing to make amends.

Learn how to mend.
I've never used a needle or thread. Mom does it in her sleep,

does everything as if today's the last day
before the dive into a bleak world of seats,
unprecedented nothingness. I've lost my five
minutes to freak out. It's not the weekend

yet. It's just the beginning of the fucking week.
How dare I swear! How dare you mend
this relationship with death! It's only fair to live five
more years. Five more decades. That's better. Sleep
it all off. If I pump my dreams and elongate them, sit
pretty, it'll feel like an everlasting day.

So here we are, five degrees hotter than last week.
Today hasn't yet had a chance to mend,
a chance to sit, a chance to sleep.

As I Am Stung by a Persistent Yellow Jacket

I shout FUUUCK at the exact moment
the neighborhood turns silent.
I convalesce for six hours
thinking, I know there's still a risk
when disposing that nest beneath the mulch,
the size of the entrance to their den tinier than a nickel,
worth more than the aphids and grubs
they destroyed all summer long.

We destroy the hornets in turn, a holy cycle.

My chives continue to thrive
even as the wettest spring morphs
into the driest summer.

I remember reading a book as a kid:
one character provoked a nest of yellow jackets
with a stick, with his foot, something like that.

A swarm swirled around him like a tornado,
the aftermath illustrated – a fully bandaged child
lying on the bed with only mouth and nose visible.

He had it coming. He did.

An exterminator assures me whatever was used to kill
the insects would not hurt my herbs.
I rinse the ever-living hell out of them anyway.
The leaves, each vein, each stem. I never see the fallout,
the corpses bundled beneath the ground, dry as dust

for the next few weeks.

I cover the quarry-like hole where the home once was,
where life vibrated within such a finite space,
what felt like the most perfect protection.

The Reclamation of Myth

I've lost track of godliness
patiently look for truth in pixels

I don't realize how warm it's been
only when asphalt bakes and the air smothers
when I'm outside for longer than ten minutes

I love it, honestly, to be willing to lose water
and heel skin for the chance to drink from the river –

it's Lethe
I've lost track of you
haven't I?

forgive the mirrors hanging all over the room
who would have thought walking
into a solitary space brings relief

when sometimes it brings unease
when sometimes it brings loneliness
when sometimes solitude is a salve

when sometimes it's a cliff
pulling you farther over the edge
even when you think
you have everything under control?

Rotation

The time will come when Earth wobbles so fiercely that overcompensation is impossible. Notice its placement, its tilting, its hanging in there, *right there*, without a way to know it's going to stay there securely for a few million years before the sun swells up beyond its present state and renders the Second Coming a moot point. Unless that *will* be the Second Coming, an inferno that makes Satan's playground mere child's play. A blistering nugget singed beyond recognition. Encompassing flames, heat, molten rock. All things melting into the air. Souls as blemish-free as a sleek new tablecloth – an afterthought along with everything else. No more thought will be left to hang our coats on when it gets too stuffy to move.

The Future

I can see eyes glossing over,
as my voice continues.
There's umbilical yearning
to return to an ecosystem where
what surrounds you is water
a submerged spot in your subconscious.

Normalcy disappears
whenever I think about
what ten years from now should be.

A barren wasteland is what
it looks like, the inevitable plunge

into chaos. But,
it won't be like that! — they say —
see how it is now. We're all good!

We're munching on lemons,
teeth pressed tightly,
our very own reamers,
and what falls down is inevitable
failure. We've failed. We knew
we had to change,
but we keep doing nothing.

We know
the future in a way
we've always known.

I Missed My Calling

I missed my calling as an antler
I knew it would be tough
to whittle things down to a point
where nothing spirals into something
can there ever be swirling candy
that wraps around me in the tethered
blank of November
ask some random orb, is this how
it's going to be for us, the lie
is set, the die is cast, and I'm back
to telling myself you can
be that fucking antler
tell it to your reflection
eyes gleaming and head spinning
as a top headed down a hill

Another End-of-the-World Poem

words spoken like a true Sibyl
informs who else is going to fall
who else will they come after

there's an Adirondack chair on the deck
leaves pile on the seat in the most lurid hues
only for one month
the air doesn't want to keep the chill

we were ordered to leap below desks
plunge into fallout shelters
with only a minute to spare
because if we do that one important thing
that silly little thing
everything will be OK

If We Go on a Trip to Portugal when We're 50…

What will we see?
Will there be a safe moment
when wildfires aren't raging across and razing
the once-lush landscape, our breaths deep
as the air thickens with smog?

It might be too late to experience Lisbon –
it's been overrun by tourists for years now
clogging the tight alleys of Baixa-Chiado
but maybe just maybe we'll find
a hidden fado bar in the midst of falsehoods
sit at tables and nibble at tremoços
and listen to a man sitting with his guitar
sharing his story of heartbreak

and maybe just maybe we'll have a little one with us
and they'll be transfixed at the strums
and the vocals in an unknown language

and the question is posed:
Daddy why is that man crying as he's singing?
and I'll look and hear the salt and pain
in each syllable and in each ask
with wet eyes from smoke and sadness
and I see myself in the beer glass reflection
yes, why is that man crying?

perhaps this is the last few moments of Portugal
perhaps this is my child's only visit
perhaps this is the last few moments of everything

and what will my breath hold
if I hold it for too long?

"What If I Told You Lemon Trees Once Existed?" takes motifs from a music video for "Graceless" by The National: putting on sunglasses, wearing tuxedos, riding a bike into a swimming pool.

"Bloodbuzz" is inspired by the song "Bloodbuzz Ohio," written and performed by The National.

"We're Humming Al Green Songs as We Get Ready for Bed" is inspired by multiple songs by Al Green. Mary and I danced to "Let's Stay Together" during our reception.

"Everything in Its Right Place" is the first song on Radiohead's album *Kid A*.

"After the Start of Summer" was inspired by the intense algae blooms on Lake Erie in August of 2014 that rendered residents of Toledo, Ohio, unable to drink or even touch their water for multiple days. In parts of Ontario, the ban lasted two weeks.

The title of "It's Easy to Lose Your Breath" is a Mondegreen of a lyric from "Wake Up Your Saints" by The National. The actual lyric is: "It's easy to lose your grip." (I like my line better.)

In the same poem, a description of the ants consuming everything alludes to Gabriel García Márquez's *One Hundred Years of Solitude*.

"Ancient Burial Ground" was inspired by the Dakota Access Pipeline protests that started in 2016.

The book with the yellow jacket scene mentioned in "As I Am Stung by a Persistent Yellow Jacket" is from a chapter in *Little House in the Big Woods* by Laura Ingalls Wilder.

And the final, most important, note: No AI was used in the creation of this poetry collection.

Acknowledgements

Earlier versions of the following poems were published in these magazines and journals:

Antonym: "It's Easy to Lose Your Breath," "Sisyphus," "There's Always a Warm Spell in February," and "What If I Told You Lemon Trees Once Existed?"

The Aurora Journal: "Alchemy"

The Bookends Review: "Rotation"

Cataloguing Poetry: "I Missed My Calling"

Feral: "The Reclamation of Myth"

Ghost City Review: "During the First Year of the Pandemic, a Frog Snuck into the House"

The Indianapolis Review: "A New Year Grows Its First Set of Teeth"

Ink Drinkers: "Breadcrumbs"

The Jupiter Review: "As I Am Stung by a Persistent Yellow Jacket"

Memoir Mixtapes: "We're Humming Al Green Songs as We Get Ready for Bed"

Moist Poetry Journal: "After the Start of Summer"

Rising Phoenix Review: "Ancient Burial Ground"

Some Words: "A Blue Jay Flies into the Window"

Thimble Literary Magazine: "Ground"

Wasteland Review: "April Tanka" and "An Icy Triptych"

"Zoom Cards Against Humanity" was included as a part of *The Second Chance Anthology*, a collection of re-homed work, published by Variant Literature in 2020.

A big thank you to RD Morgan and Sneža Žabić for reading my work, loving it, and being incredible editors and guides through the entire process. It's an honor to be read so openly and honestly, while bringing really helpful feedback and insight I didn't even notice.

Thank you also to Mitch Nobis and Jared Beloff for NAWP (if you all don't know about it, what are you waiting for – https://notatawp.com/). I love how it's brought so many poets together, those who have and haven't been to AWP. It's been an honor to be a part of and witness to so many events throughout the NAWP season, which is all the time. Thank you also for your kind insight in the past and your support – and for reading this collection and sharing your thoughts in advance.

A hearty thank you to all the folks at Variant Literature – press mates, readers, and editors – who brought me in during the start of the pandemic, and for publishing my chapbook, *Do Us A Favor*. I'm eternally grateful as a reader for the journal that I get to immerse myself in poems now and again, and hear others' thoughts as we put together issues.

There are so many other poets, writers, and musical artists that have been an inspiration to me, not just during the pandemic, but before and after. The National is the biggest, as is visible through this collection of poems.

Thank you to my family and friends who have supported me, been kind and understanding, and who were willing to hike, brunch, or whatever else with me (and Mary) during the heart of the pandemic, when we decided that inside things weren't in the cards.

I also want to say thank you to all the creatures, large and small, who wound up being a part of this menagerie of a collection. We have done such a disservice to you throughout these past few centuries in particular. And it seems that we're not stopping with our callousness. I wish we humans weren't as much of a plague.

Lastly, I want to thank my wife, Mary, for being such an inspiration to me. That first year of the pandemic was really tough, and her being there with me saved me during a time that felt so overwhelming. Mary, thank you so much for loving me, giving me support, and showing me kindness as we both navigated a very different world (especially a world that many people didn't see). You were a witness to many of the moments in this book, and you will be a witness to many others. I love you endlessly, çileğim.

About the Author

Kevin A. Risner is the author of *My Ear is a Sieve* (Bottlecap Press, 2017), *Do Us a Favor* (Variant Literature, 2021), *You Thought This Was Just Going To Be about Cleveland Didn't You?* (Ghost City Press, 2022), *It's Easy to Lose Your Breath* (Match Factory Editions, 2026), and *There's No Future Where We Don't Have Fire* (Unsolicited Press, 2027). He is a product of Ohio and has lived there most of his life, except for brief stints in England and Turkey. You can find him hiking on the trails with his wife, lounging around with a book, or hoping amongst hopes that one of his sports teams from Cleveland might someday win another championship (to prove that 2016 was no mere fluke).